God Knew

A Baby's Journey Home

written and illustrated by
Anne Lilley Becknell

Text and illustrations copyright 2011 by Anne Lilley Becknell. All rights reserved. No part of this book may be reproduced or transmitted in any form or by any means, electronic or mechanical, including photography, recording, or any information storage and retrieval system, without permission in writing from the publisher. The only exceptions are brief excerpts and reviews.

Author and Ilustrator: Anne Lilley Franklin (formerly Anne Lilley Becknell)
Copy Editor: Lynn Bemer Coble

PCKids is an imprint of **Paws and Claws Publishing, LLC.**
1589 Skeet Club Road, Suite 102-175
High Point, NC 27265
www.PawsandClawsPublishing.com
info@pawsandclawspublishing.com

ISBN #978-0-9846724-9-3
Printed in the United States

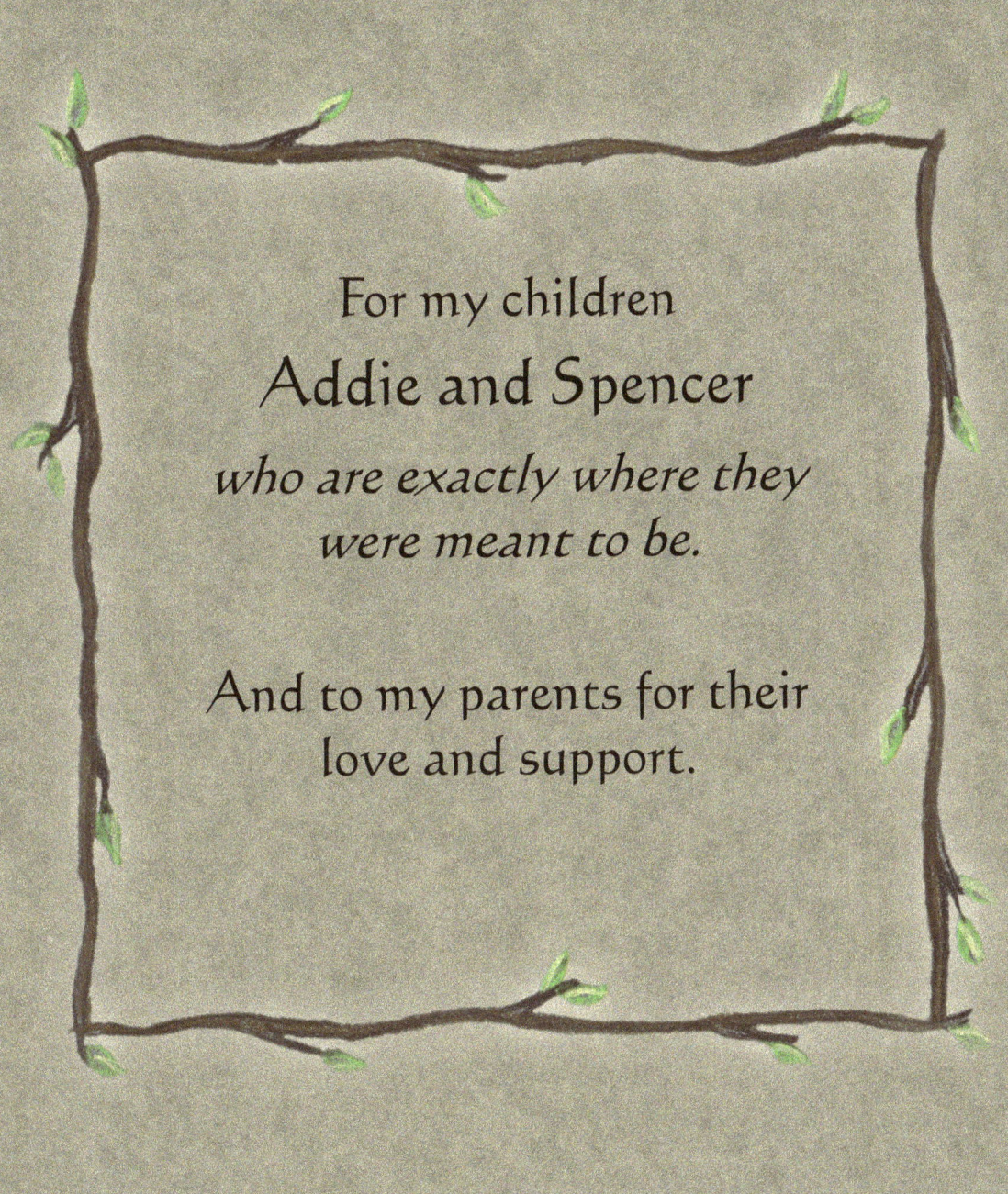

For my children
Addie and Spencer
who are exactly where they were meant to be.

And to my parents for their love and support.

In a land far away, there was a young woman with a baby in her tummy. She was all alone. She didn't know what she should do…

God knew.

The woman gave birth to a sweet, beautiful baby boy. She loved him very much but she didn't know how she could take care of him…

God knew.

The woman decided to take the baby to an orphanage. That is a place where he would be cared for until he had a home of his own.

She still didn't know if she was doing the right thing…

God knew.

On the other side of the world, a couple longed for a baby to love. They decided on adoption. They didn't know how long they would have to wait…

One day the orphanage received word that a mommy and daddy had been found for the baby. The baby did not know his parents yet...

God knew.

The baby was taken to a foster home where he would stay until time to leave for his own home.

The foster family took very good care of him, but he did not know why he kept changing homes…

God knew.

His mommy and daddy prepared a nursery for their baby's arrival. His room was filled with special gifts from family and friends. The baby did not know how many people loved him…

God knew.

The day came for the baby to travel. His foster family was sad to see him go but very happy he would have a mommy and daddy. The baby did not know where he was going…

God knew.

An escort carried the baby onto a big airplane and comforted him. There were other escorts with babies on the plane, too. They flew for a very long time. The baby didn't know that his very own family was waiting for him at the airport...

God knew.

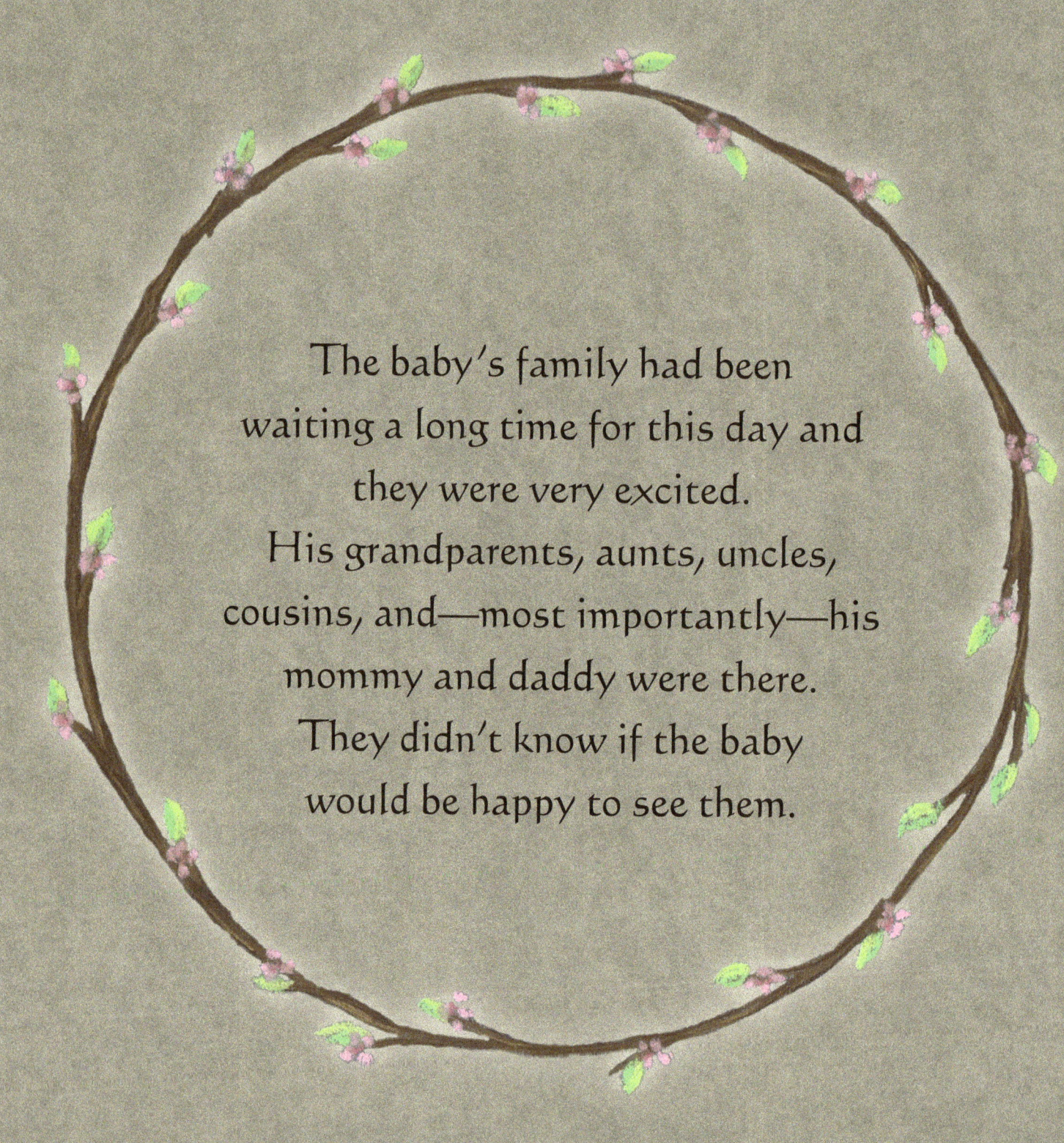

The baby's family had been waiting a long time for this day and they were very excited. His grandparents, aunts, uncles, cousins, and—most importantly—his mommy and daddy were there. They didn't know if the baby would be happy to see them.

God knew…

When the plane landed, the escort carried the baby up the walkway to his family. She put him in his mommy's arms, and he put his head on her shoulder. The baby was exactly where he belonged…

Our Journey

www.ingramcontent.com/pod-product-compliance
Lightning Source LLC
LaVergne TN
LVHW070058080426
835508LV00032B/3491